# Walk the Jesus Walk

## Jesus – our Contemporary

A six part programme
for those who wish to explore
what it means to
Live in the Way of Jesus

# John Simmonds

St Marks CRC Press Sheffield

# Together in Hope –
# Resources for Christian Faith Today

This series of resource books is the fruit of a number of organisations working together to give encouragement and hope to those who seek a credible Christian faith for the twenty first century.

We hope that these books will be helpful to those individuals and groups, inside and outside the Church, who are exploring matters of faith and belief.

We are grateful to our authors and encourage others to offer their services.

For further information about the sponsoring organisations please see the back cover. If you wish to contact the editorial group email **togetherinhope.editor@gmail.com**

The current convenor is Adrian Alker

## John Simmonds

John has served as an ordained minister in a variety of places and positions, mostly in local Methodist churches from the rural Shetland Islands to cosmopolitan West London. For thirteen years he was responsible for post-ordination training in the Methodist Church in Great Britain. His abiding passion is to invite people to take seriously the Way of Living made clear by Jesus of Nazareth. With others, he has campaigned for an inclusive church and now, in retirement, delights in conversation with people who are seeking asylum in Sheffield, a City of Sanctuary.

# A word to the reader

This little book is an attempt to introduce people to the Way of Jesus - Jesus of Nazareth, who has meant so much to so many people throughout the past two millennia.

My conviction is that the real Jesus has been taken away from us, so that we rarely catch a glimpse of the charismatic teacher and prophet who lived in Palestine about two thousand years ago. The Jesus Christ of the Church often bears little resemblance to its founder.

Is it possible to discover Jesus as he was before the Church got its hands on him? Maybe it's impossible, but one has to try. Here is my attempt to seek out the first Jesus.

Many people have inspired my search, including scholars, poets, artists, actors and movie-makers. Above all, conversations with countless numbers of people in hundreds of settings have encouraged and informed me.

Because I owe so much to so many, I cannot even begin to acknowledge which insight came from where. Profound apologies and sincere thanks to those who quickly discover that I have absorbed their ideas and represented them as if they were my own.

I have written this material because people, who cannot cope with the traditional teachings of the church, say they are still eager to explore the life and ministry of Jesus so that they might find in him an inspiration for contemporary living. This is my contribution.

I hope that people will find that the Way of Jesus inspires them to live life to the full.


John Simmonds   October 2010

# Walk the Jesus Walk

## Contents

**Walk the Jesus Walk is a programme designed for people who wish to discover what it means to follow the Way of Jesus.**

The programme will help us:

**Unearth** what it meant to be followers of Jesus in his day.

What impact did he have on their lives?

What did they expect; what did they get?

What did they find inspiring and challenging?

**Discover** what it means to be followers of Jesus today.

What impact does Jesus' chosen way of life have on us?

Is this similar or different from his impact on the first followers?

**Identify** what practical commitments we might have to make if we chose to be his followers.

**The programme can be used individually or in a group**. However it would be most helpful for readers to talk to one another to share ideas and experiences. It could also be helpful to invite an experienced group leader to facilitate conversations. The programme might be useful in a youth group, house group, confirmation/membership or Lent group.

Although there are six sections in this programme, groups need not be tied to one section per session.

# 1 My story, my journey

In this first session, we recognise that each person has both a distinctive personality and a unique experience of life. These will affect how we approach the stories of Jesus and how we will respond to his words and actions. Different people will react in different ways. So, in this section, we take time to consider the influences which have made us the people we are.

**It's important to realize that our decisions and beliefs are affected....**

by the sort of people we are,

by the experiences we've had,

and by the kind of people with whom we live.

There's nothing wrong in that, but remember that it is so.

**We are all made up of a combination of . . . .**

- *Hereditary factors*

    passed on from our forebears (not only physical attributes, like the colour of our skin, but also our attitudes and ideas)

- *Environmental factors*

    coming to us from our neighbourhood, friendships, internet, TV, radio, nationality, etc.

- *A real independent self*

    the 'real me', who can either accept or resist hereditary and environmental pressures.

When we think about the meaning of life and about how to live as a Christian, it will depend in part upon the kind of people we are.

**So we begin by looking in the mirror!**

Use the following questions and see if you can discover who you are,

what made you the kind of person you are

what you expect of life, and what life demands of you

1. What is your name (proper name and nicknames)? Why are you called by these names?

2. Who belongs to your social group / family (those in your house and those who live away)?

3. What do/did other people expect of you?
   Your parents, grandparents, siblings?
   Friends and neighbours?
   Teachers, employers, colleagues?
   The government?

4. What do you expect of other people? (use the same list again)

5. Are your ambitions for yourself the same as other people's for you?

6. What are your dreams (and your nightmares !) ......
   for yourself?
   for your country?
   for the world?

7. What makes you happy?

8. What upsets you?

9. Make a list of people whom you admire, and explain why you admire them.

10. Here is the hardest question of all! What sort of person are you?
    Do you have fixed ideas?
    Do get on well with other people?
    Are you adaptable?  How do you react to the unexpected?
    Are you hard-working?
    Are you a fighter?  Will you put yourself out for something you really want?
    Are you generous?

11. Now!
    Do other people agree with your answers to question 10?

How does all this affect your faith story?

---

**Two things to do and share**

Try drawing a 'time-line' of your life, with ups and downs indicating times when you felt good or not-so-good. Indicate what happened around those times.

Take a piece of paper.

On one side write the names of people who matter to you, the closest at the centre. On the other side, write down the possessions, which you would want to keep at all cost, the most precious at the centre.

**Share your findings with others.**

---

# 2 Finding out more about Jesus

In the first chapter we recognised that each of us has a distinctive life story and personality. This means that we may respond in different ways to what Jesus said and did. In this chapter we explore where we can find the story of Jesus.

Christianity is based on the life of Jesus. It's a movement inspired by a man who lived in Palestine during the Roman occupation.

## Who was He?

Some say, 'He was a very special man who had a wonderful way with people.'

Some say, 'He was God alive on earth.'

Some say, 'He was a prophet, with remarkable insights into life and a passion for justice'.

Christians have had many disagreements; their beliefs and experiences have been very diverse; yet they have all agreed that Jesus of Nazareth is supremely important in our search for meaning and in our attempt to know God.

However, we must be careful to check whether our own views are reasonable or not. It's all too easy to invent the kind of Jesus we want! So we must look back into history to see what we can discover.

## Where can we look?

### 1. The letters of Paul

It is generally agreed that Jesus' own companions did not leave behind detailed accounts of him. The earliest written references to Jesus are in the letters of Paul even though Paul himself never met Jesus.

The first that we hear of Paul is as a fierce opponent of the early Christians. He was involved in a minor way in the stoning of Stephen, the first Christian martyr. The Acts of the Apostles has an account of his conversion and subsequently of his missionary journeys around the eastern Mediterranean. Paul was a champion of Gentile Christians (i.e. those who are not Jews); he argued that it was not necessary to become a Jew before you became a Christian. Although he is often remembered as the man who thought women should keep quiet in church, in fact in many respects he saw more clearly than anyone else in his day the consequences of the life, teaching, death and resurrection of Jesus.

Remarkably, Paul says very little about the life of Jesus and quotes hardly anything that Jesus said. He says much more about the risen Christ, who appeared to him on the Damascus road. However, if we look through the letters he wrote to the young churches which he helped to found, we do see a number of references to Jesus, particularly to the Last Supper and the Resurrection. Here are the most important of them, taken from various letters:

- He was descended from David according to the flesh and designated Son of God in power by his resurrection from the dead. (Romans 1:3)

- He died for our sins in accordance with the Scriptures, he was buried, he was raised on the third day in accordance with the Scriptures, and he appeared to Cephas (Peter), then to the Twelve. Then he appeared to more than five hundred brethren at one time, most of whom are still alive, though some have fallen asleep. (I Corinthians 15: 3-6)

- On the night when he was betrayed, he took bread, and when he had given thanks, he broke it and said, 'This is my body which is for you. Do this in remembrance of me.' In the same way also the cup, after supper, saying, 'This cup is the new covenant in my blood. Do this, as often as you drink it, in remembrance of me.'(I Corinthians 11: 23-25)

- I saw none of the other Apostles except James the Lord's brother. (Galatians 1:19)

## 2 The New Testament Gospels

Some years after Paul, the first Gospels were written. They contain a good deal of material which had been handed down either by word of mouth or in other documents, but this was not brought together in the Gospels until a generation after Jesus' death. Of the four Gospels, Matthew, Mark and Luke belong quite closely together and are often called the 'Synoptics'; John is different in many ways and stands somewhat apart.

Mark's gospel was written first; then Matthew and Luke wrote theirs, copying many sections from Mark almost word for word. Matthew and Luke also both include material which was not in Mark. Some scholars call this shared material 'Q'; it contains many of Jesus' sayings. However, because each writer had his own interests, he would make alterations here and there. It is apparent also that each writer created new material as he developed his own understanding of Jesus.

Here are some important facts about the Gospels.

a.  The Gospels were written by Christians - that is, people who were committed to following Jesus and his Way. They are not newspaper reports or impartial histories (if you can have such things), but portraits, concerned to draw out the meaning of Jesus' life, death and resurrection. Each writer produces a distinctive portrait of Jesus by the way in which he arranges his material and the details he stresses. (See how many more of the sayings of Jesus appear in Matthew and Luke than in Mark.)

b.  None of the writers told the whole story. Whilst a great deal of material appears in more than one Gospel, much only appears in one place. (Look for yourself and see if you can find parables told only by Luke or miracles described only by John. )

    John's Gospel stands very much apart in this respect, as you can see from his version of Jesus' last supper with his friends (John 13). Here John includes Jesus washing his disciples' feet but does not include the account of Jesus sharing the bread and wine with his friends.

c.  In the portraits they painted, the Gospel writers not only wanted to tell their audience about what Jesus said and did. They were concerned about two other things:

    i   Jesus was the fulfilment of the hopes and promises of the Jewish scriptures (the Old Testament), the Bible of his own people, the Jews.

    ii  Hearing stories about Jesus would help people to follow in his way.

## 3 Other Gospels

As time goes on, all kinds of stories cluster around famous figures and Jesus was no exception. Many other 'Gospels' appeared during the second century, some of them obviously little more than popular entertainment or aimed at showing that Jesus was 'the greatest'. You can find these collected together in what is called The Apocryphal New Testament. We are told how, for example, Jesus cursed a child who bumped into him in the street, whereupon the child dropped down dead; or how Jesus would help Joseph by stretching planks which Joseph had cut too short!

Other 'apocryphal' Gospels are best understood as ways in which groups of new Christians tried to make sense of Jesus in terms of their own different experience and culture. One collection of such Gospels, so-called 'Gnostic Gospels', were found in 1945 in Nag Hammadi, in Egypt, having been lost since the second century AD. They show how some Christians attempted to interpret Jesus in a more 'spiritual' way.

## 4 Christians through Roman eyes

Almost all our information about Jesus comes from Christians, both those in dominant groups and those on the fringe. In the early days of Christianity there would have been little cause for non-Christian writers to mention him. However, there are some allusions in Roman literature.

*Tacitus*, writing about AD 116 of the persecution of Christians by Nero, regards the followers of Jesus and their religion as a 'pernicious superstition'. He tells us that their leader, Christus, was executed by Pontius Pilate in the reign of Tiberius.

*Suetonius*, a biographer of the same period, tells us that Claudius expelled the Jews from Rome because they constantly caused disturbances 'at the instigation of Chrestus'.

*Pliny*, a contemporary Roman governor, asks his emperor how to deal with Christians singing hymns to Christ 'as to a god'.

## 5 2000 years of translating and story-telling

Over the past two thousand years, the story of Jesus has been retold in hundreds of languages and by millions of people. Bible translators, preachers, teachers and authors have all played their part. Jesus has been portrayed in mystery plays, stained glass windows, religious art, comic strips, hymns, plays and novels. So much so that we can easily forget that no-one knows what Jesus looked like.

Whilst in some ways he will remain a mystery, there is still a good chance that his life can still influence ours for good. That's why people keep writing songs and painting pictures, telling stories and preaching sermons. Recall Sydney Carter's famous lines in Lord of the Dance:

'they buried my body, they thought I'd gone,

but I am the dance and I still go on.'

## To sum up

What we know about Jesus and the first Christians comes from the New Testament, most prominent in which are the Gospels and the letters of Paul.

Once we begin to look further at the story of Jesus and the growth of the church, we find that it is quite complicated and that we do not know all the details.

What is in the New Testament is influenced
-by the character, convictions and aims of the writers;
-by the different environments in which they worked;
-by their subject - Jesus: risen from death; fulfilling Old Testament hopes; initiating God's Kingdom.

Although some details of what happened may be unclear, what we do see are writers who have put their faith in Jesus as the one who announced a new age - the Kingdom of God - to be realized here and now; calling people to change their ways by allowing God to govern their lives. Everyone had cause to celebrate because the reign of God was arriving. And yet, God demanded total obedience and his claims were paramount. Above all, Jesus was not just a person from the past, he was a living Lord to be followed now.

And remember, each one of us will read the story of Jesus through our own eyes and according to our own experience of life.

---

**Things to do and share**

1. Try to recall the ways in which you have learnt about Jesus. What images of Jesus did you grow up with?
2. What are the most important things you would say about Jesus to an enquirer?

---

# 3 What Jesus stood for

**Recap**

In the first session we recognised that each person has a unique character and experience of life. Both will affect how they approach the stories of Jesus and how they will respond to his words and actions. In the second session we explored how we can find out more about him.

**In this section we identify some of the convictions that were central to Jesus' way of life** - beliefs and attitudes which bear upon our lives and demand a response from us.

**• Jesus believed that this is God's world and everyone matters**

Jesus believed that everything and everyone is God's business (Matt 5: 38-48)

This means that everyone is a child of God - even people we don't like. We belong to one another. There's more to life than simply pursuing personal ends.

*How might all this affect the way you live and how you relate to other people?*

**• Jesus had an unusual bunch of friends**

They were not all fishermen! They included

- a patriotic freedom fighter, Simon the Zealot (Mark 3:18)
- a man who collected taxes for the Roman occupying forces (Matt. 9.9)
- women, with various stories (Luke 8: 1-3)

Jesus spent time with many kinds of people, even unsavoury and unpopular characters, as well as needy people (Luke 5: 27-32). Yet he was sought out by leaders, rich and respectable people - even an army captain and a synagogue leader (Luke 7:1-10; Luke 8: 40-42,49-56).

*Are contemporary churches and Christians open to all kinds of people?*

*Can you think of anyone with whom you would have difficulty?*

*(see 'Something to think about' at the end of this section)*

**• Jesus believed that there is a purpose in life**

God's will is that people should live in unity and peace with one another and be willing to forgive those who harm them.

Jesus talked about the 'kingdom of God', i.e. the rule of God. So we work and pray for a day when God's will shall be done 'on earth as in heaven' (Matt 6: 9-13).

*In what ways have people helped to bring about 'the kingdom of God'?*

*In what ways have we thwarted the coming of 'the kingdom of God'?*

### • Jesus had a distinctive life-style

His stories show his delight in observing the ways of men and women.

He believed that life is to be enjoyed (Luke 5: 33-39).

He enjoyed parties and meals (Luke 19: 5; Mark 2: 15-17).

On the other hand Jesus took little pleasure in material wealth. Riches would not secure a person's future. 'If you want to learn from me,' he said, 'then forget yourself and follow me'. (Mark 10: 17-25)

*Is it possible for you, as a 21st century Western person, to copy Jesus' distinctive life-style?*

*How, in practice, would you go about it?*

### • Jesus cared for people

This was the hallmark of Jesus' life. The well-being of others was supremely important; more so than rules and regulations. People with all kinds of problems turned to him for help. His selfless love was infectious (Mark 10: 46-52; Luke 8: 40-56).

*Which individuals and groups around you care for others in the way Jesus did?*

*What place does concern for others have in your daily life?*

### • Jesus called God 'Abba'

It was a surprise to the Jews to hear Jesus call God 'Abba' (usually translated 'father'). The nearest word we have to 'Abba' is 'Daddy' or 'Dad'. The Jews believed that God is unapproachable yet Jesus treated God as a constant companion, to whom he looked for strength. (Luke 11: 1-4). At crucial moments in his life, Jesus took time out to think and pray, for prayer was a natural part of his life.

*How do you react to Jesus' idea of God? Do you have another view?*

### • Jesus was ready to suffer for what he believed

The friends of Jesus found it hard to accept that following him meant self-denial and even suffering. Again and again Jesus failed to get them to understand what he really stood for. He was not a powerful princely figure, but rather a servant, unprotected from exploitation and abuse. (Mark 10: 35-45)

*List some people who have followed a 'way of suffering'.*

*Describe a situation in which to remain faithful to the way of Jesus you might have to suffer.*

**This way of Jesus is no soft option. It's costly.**

It's the way Jesus lived himself; here is how Jesus has been described:

*'He was sincere in all he did; he knew what he stood for; he could put up with anything; he was very kind; he didn't just talk about loving people, he actually succeeded in loving them; he always told people the plain truth; but he knew God was with him and trusted God's power'.* (Alan Dale)

Living like that led to execution for Jesus on a Roman cross. But afterwards the disciples discovered that the secret of life was to live as he had lived, selflessly, sacrificially, lovingly (Philippians 2: 2-16).

Don't be persuaded to believe that following the way of Jesus is simple and straightforward. We will sometimes wonder whether we are doing the right thing. We may feel really alone but this can be the cost of discipleship.

---

**Something to think about**

**Given the kind of person you are, in what ways is it easy or hard for you to see Jesus as a contemporary – a person who can affect your life today?**

For example, is it really possible to be open to everyone or to include everyone? How about people who deliberately harm others, e.g. those who abuse children, torture prisoners or traffic young women?

Jesus said that God sends sunshine and rain on good people and bad people alike (Matt 6:43-48). So everyone benefits from God's generous love. Yet Jesus had harsh things to say about some people, especially those who made other people suffer. He was often critical of rich people because they made poor people suffer (Luke 16: 19-31).

It is as though Jesus is saying, whilst God longs to surround all people in a loving embrace, God is deeply distressed when people exclude one another.

*Describe any attitudes and actions which you find hard to tolerate.*

*How should we approach people who behave in intolerant ways?*

# 4 Jesus and his friends

## Recap

In the first session we recognised that each of us has our own personality and experience of life, which we bring into our journey as a disciple of Jesus. All kinds of influences have made us the people we are.

In the second session we sought to find out more about Jesus, especially in the Bible.

In the third session we recognised that, for every Christian, Jesus of Nazareth is of crucial importance. We identified some of the convictions that were central to Jesus' way of life  - beliefs and attitudes which call for a response from us today.

**In this session,** we look deeper into what it meant for the first disciples to follow Jesus and what it might mean for us today.

## 1.He said 'Follow me'

Jesus came, almost out of nowhere, to a variety of ordinary people, and interrupted what they were doing. He came to the fishermen, Peter, Andrew, James and John, on the lakeshore, and summoned them to fish for people. He came to Matthew, the tax collector, and to half a dozen or so others,  and to all of them said, 'Follow me' (Mark 1 14-19; 2:13-14).   He challenged them to leave their homes and families and to join him on the road.

Jesus' words challenge people today - men and women, no matter what they may be doing, and the call is the same: 'Follow me'.

*Have you had an experience of being 'interrupted' by the challenge of Jesus, or being made to think differently or do something new?*

## 2.He offered them a great deal

Jesus wanted people to enjoy life at its best, responding to the love of God. Through teaching and healing, he brought hope, life and wholeness, when the world around seemed under the dominion of death, demons and decay.

When people were with him, life was often like a party, and he was often to be found at meals given by others (John 2: 1-12; Luke 7: 36-50).

He did not hold himself back in any way. In the end, what he offered to people was no less than himself (Luke 22: 14-20).

*Which words of Jesus mean the most to you and why?*

### 3. He asked a great deal of them

Jesus challenged people to turn away from evil and to allow God to govern their lives.

He encouraged them to care deeply for one another, to forgive those who hurt them, and to love both neighbours and enemies (Matt 5: 43-47; 18, 21-35).

He knew they didn't understand everything. In fact, what he asked was so hard that they constantly misunderstood, even after quite a long time; yet they remained disciples (Matt 20: 20-28).

He didn't only call respectable people; in fact he said that they didn't need him. He was concerned for the disreputable - and that wasn't easy to take (Mark 2: 16-17).

*Describe how Jesus challenges the way we live our lives today.*

### 4. He spent a lot of time with them

'Following' really meant going where he led them — around and about in Galilee, south to Jerusalem and beyond. They listened hard and long to his words; they observed his ways; they learned to draw strength from him (Mark 3: 13-19).

*How do you focus on being 'a friend of Jesus' today? What approach do you find helpful?*

### 5. He involved them in his work

He gave them jobs to do, tackling the evil powers at work in the world; superstition, greed, disease. So, even when they were not at his side, they were following his instructions and his example (Mark 6: 7-12).

*What kind of work might we be involved in?*

*Make a list of different kinds of compassionate action which you have heard about. Do you know of any local examples?*

*What do you do yourself?*

## 6. He shared special meals with them

Jesus and his disciples shared many meals with people. His first followers told of the Passover meal (The Last Supper) they shared on the evening before Jesus was arrested. As he handed them the bread and wine, it was as though Jesus was giving himself to them. (see *The Last Supper* below)

---

**Something to think about**

Can you think of something which sums up what it means to follow Jesus today?

A story, picture, song, or whatever?

---

**The Last Supper**

Down the centuries, Jesus' followers have re-enacted this meal. Each time, they sought to strengthen their relationship with Jesus as their leader and example. In one of the earliest parts of the New Testament, Paul describes how this special meal symbolises their corporate life (I Cor. 11: 27-33) . Here, he says that, when at the Lord's Supper greedy people grab all the food and leave poor people to go hungry, they sin against the very body and blood of Jesus.

Christians still respond to Jesus' invitation to eat bread and drink wine 'in remembrance' of him. This meal is known by many names: e.g. Lord's Supper, Eucharist, Holy Communion, Mass, Breaking of Bread. Such names reflect the enormous differences in the way the meal is celebrated – sometimes with extravagant liturgy and ceremony, sometimes with very few words and actions. Church buildings, elaborate or simple, provide a theatrical setting for this service.

Christians have very different beliefs about communion, about who can receive the bread and wine, and about who can lead (celebrate at) the service.

Sometimes this meal has united Christians, often it has bitterly divided them; some Christians do not have a special meal, because they believe that every meal is a gift of God, when Jesus is present.

*What do you think of this 'meal'?*

*Which of the names would you give it?*

*What it the best way to re-enact this meal today?*

---

# 5 Following in the Way

**Recap**

**In the first session,** we recognised that each person has a unique experience of life, which is brought into our journey as disciples of Jesus. All kinds of influences have made people what they are.

**In the second session,** we noted where we might discover more about Jesus.

**In the third session,** we recognised that Jesus of Nazareth is of crucial importance. We identified some of the convictions that were central to his way of life.

**In the fourth session,** we looked deeper into what it meant for the first disciples to follow Jesus and what it could mean for us today.

**In this session**

We consider how we might shape a way of life for ourselves as followers in the Way of Jesus.

- **Many people believe that there is more to reality than the visible, tangible experiences of life.** Along with religious people of every age and culture, they talk about the activity of God - in themselves, in others, in the world. In this way they attempt to make sense of the world and explore the principles that might guide and explain human affairs and destinies.

- **Talking about God is not peculiar to Christians;** what distinguishes them is their relationship to Jesus of Nazareth (about 6BCE – 30CE). However, they would not all describe this relationship in the same way:

  - Some emphasise individual and personal experiences of 'Jesus – alive today!' They claim direct contact with him, through conversion, prayer and the Bible.

  - Some have a close affinity with the attitudes and values which Jesus set out in his teaching and demonstrated by his actions.

  - Some believe that the church today possesses special insights and powers which were given to the first Christians by Jesus, and have been passed on down the centuries.

- **All believe that, in some way, Jesus helps them understand the meaning of life,** by teaching them about God and how they should respond to God.

- **Unfortunately, from the very beginning, some people have claimed to be the 'true' Christians.** In the conviction that they alone are right, they have outlawed one another, and indeed persecuted those who disagreed with them. Thus new churches came to be formed. Today, Christians still find it impossible to agree on many things.

**And yet, even in their disagreements they have something in common;** they all claim to have special knowledge of Jesus. For it is in the process of defining what they believe about Jesus that they squabble! Why do Christians come to different conclusions? It has something to do with:

- who they are and what circumstances they live in;
- how they read the Bible;
- how they respond to what other Christians say;
- what really matters to them at the time; and so on .....

*What factors influence the way you think about God and Jesus? (think back to session 1)*

- **Our search will be closely related to our understanding of God.**

The traditional Jewish / Christian / Muslim view is that God is the Final Controller of everything: people, planets and galaxies. This is a God who is above, beyond and outside us. It uses specific names to describe God, like Creator, Eternal, All-Knowing, Almighty, Lord, King, Judge, and so on. Many human institutions have mirrored such beliefs about what God is like, e.g. emperor, king, priest, father, the State. Many people believe that, in adopting a position of power and control, the church has lost touch with the Jesus of the Gospels.

- **But what about Jesus' understanding of God? His raison d'être?**

**One of the most precious possessions of the Christian tradition is the 'Lord's Prayer'.** Luke tells us in ch.11: 1- 4 that Jesus' followers asked him to teach them how to pray. This prayer gives us an insight into Jesus' understanding of God.

- He calls God 'Abba', an intimate first utterance made as an infant attempts to connect with its parent. The child is responding to love as it mutters 'abba-abba-abba', ma-ma-ma or da-da-da (Our Father).
- He stresses how important God is in his life – how he puts God at the centre (May your name be honoured).
- He longs for God's wishes to be realised across the world (May your kingdom come).

- He asks for enough food for each day (Give us today our daily bread).
- He wishes to be compassionate to other people just as God is compassionate to him (Forgive us, as we forgive).
- He seeks the strength to survive the vagaries of life (Save us from times of trial).

**In our imagination, we might also ask 'Jesus, teach us to pray'.** In the conviction that God is Love, he might reply:

- Respond to Love wherever Love is to be found.
- Let this Love possess you fully; keep Love at the centre of your thoughts and actions.
- Allow this Love to flow far and wide, stimulating compassionate actions and creating just relationships.
- Eat enough but not too much; consume wisely, not greedily.
- God will be patient and kind to you when you mess things up; try to be the same towards those who upset you.
- Hang in there when life gets tough!  I'll stick by you.

So we have a blueprint for our own prayers.

### How did Jesus view his own vocation?

Luke says that Jesus was energised by God's Spirit. This spirit brought about his birth (1:35), came down to him at his baptism (3:22), guided him (4:1) sustained him (4:14), set the agenda for his life's work (4:18).  In his first public address, he sets out his programme:

The Spirit of the Lord is upon me because he has chosen me to bring good news to the poor.

He has sent me to proclaim liberty to captives and recovery of sight to the blind;

to set free the oppressed;

and announce that the time has come when the Lord will save his people. (Luke 4: 18-19)

It follows from this that any group or individual, claiming to be following in the Way of Jesus will engage in a similar programme.

*How does Jesus' programme translate into 21st century terms?*

*Imagine and describe a church which is 'Good News to the Poor'.*

**Take some time out to read through Mark 10: 35-45**

Note that the natural inclination of James and John is to grasp at powerful seats in the coming kingdom. Jesus explains that he is advocating a new style of leadership, one that is unlike secular models. They must aspire to be slaves, not masters - for he himself 'came not to be served but to serve.'

*So how come that, by and large, the church prefers to copy the rulers of this world rather than to adopt the posture of Jesus?*

# 6 Living it out - a Programme for Tomorrow

**Something to think about before going further**

**In this series, you have been bombarded with questions...**

about yourself.....your group.....the world.....Jesus.....your beliefs.....the church.....
.....and so on..... *Questions.....questions.....questions!*

**A mature person** is someone who can live with the questions which life brings, rather than run away from them - even when there are no simple answers. Such a person can:

• face uncertainty with hope

• act confidently, even when the way ahead is unclear

• follow the way of Jesus, without always understanding everything

• find strength to live positively, even when stress and suffering have to be endured

**Similarly, a mature church or group** is one which lives creatively with questions: it's an 'enquiring community' of people committed to the search for greater understanding. Here people will find sympathy, tolerance and acceptance but not necessarily agreement. Argument, and even conflict, can be fruitful and creative. To stifle disagreement is to stunt growth and restrict development.

*Are you prepared to change to accommodate other people? Or do you expect them to fit in with your ideas?*

*How best can we work together even when we differ on serious issues?*

There are times when attitudes are more important than ideas and dogmas (See Philippians 2: 1-11).

## Recap

**In the first session,** we recognised that each of us has our own experience of life, which we bring into our journey as a disciple of Jesus. All kinds of influences have made us the people we are.

**In the second session,** we considered the various sources from which the story of Jesus comes.

**In the third session,** we recognised that, for every Christian, Jesus of Nazareth is of crucial importance. We identified some of the convictions that were central to Jesus' way of life - beliefs and attitudes which demand a response from us today.

**In the fourth session,** we looked into what it meant for the first disciples to follow Jesus and what it could mean for us today.

**In the fifth session** we looked closer at Jesus' deepest convictions and how they impact on our attitude to God and God's world.

**Now we search for a 'Programme for Tomorrow'** – what it means in practice to live in the Way of Jesus.

If we proceed towards tomorrow in a spirit of discovery, we may find that we have to revise some of our assumptions.

**• How can we best talk about Jesus?**

In a way which is true for us but which is also true to him and will mean something to other people?

**• How can the church best respond to the message of Jesus?**

In its worship celebrations?

*What about its liturgies (i.e. forms of service, hymns, prayers, etc)?*

*Are they intelligible? Do they say the right things?*

*Has tradition become an end in itself?*

*Do we need different kinds of worship for different people?*

In its activities?

*Do we spend our time doing the right things?*

*What ought we to be doing for one another, and for other people, near and far?*

In its organization?

*Who makes the plans and takes the decisions? Does everyone feel involved?*

*Do the buildings, committees, and functions help people to live in the way of Jesus?*

*How is the church's money obtained and spent?*

*Have we got our priorities right?*

**• How does following Jesus affect the way we live?**

*the company we keep?*

*how we earn our money?*

*how we use it. . . house, car, holidays, other people, the poor?*

**The big question about tomorrow is...**

*Is the way of Jesus significant enough to change things for you, your group, your church, your world?*

**If the answer is 'yes',**

then start writing a programme for tomorrow ......

**A programme prompted by God's Spirit,**

the spirit that filled Jesus - the one who makes God real:

creatively working in the world - making new things happen - active in human life;

renewing our strength and our hope, binding us to one another.

**It will mean**

**- A personal commitment to live life in the spirit of Jesus**

*to go on seeking answers to your questions*

*and the fulfilment of your aspirations;*

*to which you can give yourself honestly and completely.*

**- A commitment to others**

*joining with them to celebrate the love of God;*

*to learn together about the way of Jesus;*

*to support one another at all times; to share in Christian work.*

**- A commitment to the world and its people**

*some enjoy its riches and its beauty;*

*others wait in misery for a better day.*

**- A commitment to the way of Jesus**

*acknowledging that this is God's world;*

*seeking a purpose in life;*

*enjoying an unusual bunch of friends;*

*living life thoughtfully and using resources carefully;*

*caring about people;*

*loving wastefully as God loves;*

*even if it means being uncomfortable.*

# Further Resources

**Search on the web:** there are all kinds of material to explore, including
Article on Wikipedia, entitled Race of Jesus
*Jesus Mafa* – pictures of Jesus from an African context (www.jesusmafa.com)
Living the Questions: (www.livingthequestions.com)

**Drama:** so much to try, but take a look at
*Jesus and Peter,* sketches by John Bell and Graham Maule: published by Wild
Goose Publications and other sketches from the Iona Community.

**Pictures** from thousands of artists down the ages, including
The Methodist Church Art Collection on
www.methodistchurch.org.uk/static/artcollection
Images of Christ: Seeing Salvation Catalogue: National Gallery (look for a
second-hand paper-back edition on www.abebooks.co.uk or on
www.amazon.co.uk)
*Jesus Mafa:* see above

**Liturgy and Worship:** so many ideas out there including
Material from the Iona Community's Wild Goose Worship Group:
www.ionacommunity.com
Also anthologies by Geoffrey Duncan, Donald Hilton and Ruth Duck

### Suggestions for Further Reading

John L. Bell,
*Ten Things they never told me about Jesus* (2009)

Marcus J. Borg,
*Jesus: Uncovering the Life, Teachings, and Relevance of a Religious Revolutionary*
(2008)

Marcus J. Borg,
*Meeting Jesus Again for the First Time* (1995)

David Boulton,
*Who on Earth was Jesus?* (2008)

John Dominic Crossan,
*Jesus: A Revolutionary Biography,* (1995)

John Simmonds
*Jesus: Then and Now* (expected 2011)

John Shelby Spong,
*Jesus for the Non-Religious* (2007)